## *Introduction*

A few decades ago, being a writer was much harder and it wasn't as profitable as it is today. Generally, all the famous writers have "become rich" after they passed away – their legacy was what mattered the most.

Well, all of that has changed entirely, and being a writer is much, much easier, thanks to the expansion of the Internet – you can now connect with your readers from around the world and all of them are just 1 click away from you. This has had a huge impact for writers, publishers, artists, and enthusiasts.

As real book stores still exist, physical books continue to be bought by people who prefer to feel real paper instead of a digital screen.

If you are willing to publish a book, you have multiple options – Amazon, Barnes & Noble (Nook), Apple, SmashWords, etc.

The major player of this game is Amazon and its affiliates, and one of the most important ones is CreateSpace (Publishing on demand).

# Chapter 1: Making Money with CreateSpace

Nowadays, people prefer to buy digital eBooks instead of physical ones because it's faster, cheaper, environmentally friendly, and you theoretically have unlimited stock. However, there still are people who prefer physical books and they pay for them even though they're more expensive.

You can publish just on CreateSpace or you can publish on both Kindle and CreateSpace (I recommend doing both).

CreateSpace is the best way to convert your digital books into physical ones and it also has excellent royalty rates (they depend on the features of the book – length, cover, paper quality, etc.).

If you are already running a Kindle business, CreateSpace will give you an extra 20-30% income and you can do that completely free. So, if you have 10 Kindle books and you're making $1,000 a month, you should expect $200 - $300 more just from CreateSpace.

CreateSpace doesn't charge you anything extra unless you want to pay for a couple of premium features such as professional cover, from $399 or professional formatting, from $199. They give you a free CreateSpace assigned ISBNs, and they help you out with the whole process.

I will guide you step by step through the whole process and I will explain every detail.

# Chapter 2: Signing Up with CreateSpace

To get started, go to http://createspace.com and sign up. Use your email and choose a new password.

Before you can start publishing (uploading a new book), you first have to complete the *Tax Interview* (just like you did for KDP). For those who don't know, you need to provide tax information – where you live, what you do, if you are a U.S. or non-U.S. resident and at the end, you will receive a percentage (10-30%) of withholding rate.

U.S. and CA citizens will pay 15%, non-U.S. residents will pay 30% with small exceptions, if the country has tax treaties with the USA. For example, UK residents pay 0% withholding rates and I pay 10%

in Romania (tax treaties). Unless you don't provide an ITIN or a Social Security Number, you will pay 30% withholding rate (it will automatically be paid by CreateSpace or by Amazon).

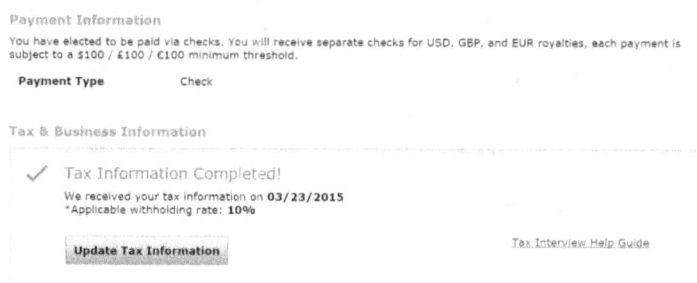

Don't be jealous if you think 0% or 10% is less than 30% or 15%, because I have to pay other local taxes, too. For those who pay 30%, you can collect the payments and ask the U.S. IRS to refund part of the taxes as you are not a U.S. citizen.

So, after you complete the whole *Tax Interview*, you are ready to upload your new titles.

# Chapter 3: Getting Paid from CreateSpace

As a member of CreateSpace, you have 2 main options of getting paid; it's basically the same system used in KDP.

**Check payment** – Unless you live in the U.S. or UK, you might not have another possibility of getting your money through direct deposit, so your only remaining option is through check deposit.

The biggest inconvenience with check payments is the fact that you need to wait until you exceed the minimum thresholds, which are 100 EUR, 100 USD, or 100 GBP.

Another thing that may annoy you is that you need to wait 1 month after you meet the minimum threshold (clearance period) until they finally send you the check.

Also, CreateSpace sends you the check at the end of each month (27-29th).

So, for example, if you make $100 in January, the next 30 days will be the clearance period, so your check will be sent on 29th February and you will get it somewhere between 5th and 10th March.

In some countries (like mine), the check policies really, *really* suck. I have to pay 10% commission to get the money, not all the banks accept checks, and I have to wait between 6 and 8 weeks to finally get my money.

It's very frustrating, especially in the beginning. My first months on CreateSpace were like this – $40-$50/month, so I had to wait 2 months to meet the threshold, 1 month clearance period, 2 weeks until the check arrived at my home and 8 weeks until I got my money.

So, in other words, from $112 sales I got a $101.4 check, for which I paid $10.14 commission and I waited 5 and a half months to get my money (from the first sale until I saw my money).

So, guys, if you're planning to get rich quickly... I'm sorry, you won't.

Although CreateSpace is a great way to increase your income using your existing books or if you enjoy writing, it won't make you rich overnight.

Of course, when you will have 30 great titles over the years, then yes, you should expect several thousands of dollars per month.

***Direct Deposit*** – If you are lucky enough to be accepted for direct deposit, things work a lot faster; I would say 3 times faster.

You only need to wait for the clearance period and then you'll see the money in your bank account.

### *Royalties*

Unlike Kindle, customers need to pay a higher price to get a print copy of the exactly same book.

Your royalty will be somewhere around 30%, so for a $9.99 book with 100 pages, you will earn about $2.64-$3.24 (if the book is Black & White).

Every time a book is printed, you earn a royalty for that.

Don't worry if you get a refund, customers usually buy your book, read it once or twice, and they return it for one reason or another.

However, the good news is that you still keep your royalty, because the book was printed, but you won't get another royalty if someone purchases a used book that has been already created.

## Chapter 4: Uploading a Book – Guided

Uploading a paperback book on CreateSpace can be done quite easily and you have two ways: **Guided** or **Expert.**

If you have never used CreateSpace before or it's the first time seeing this menu, I highly suggest you to use the Guided step-by-step process until you get familiar with it. The expert mode is a lot faster and it basically puts all the pages in a single one. I will take an example from my own book, which is called *Evernote in 90 Minutes or Less.*

### Step 1

Click "Add new title" on the home page and then you will start the whole process.

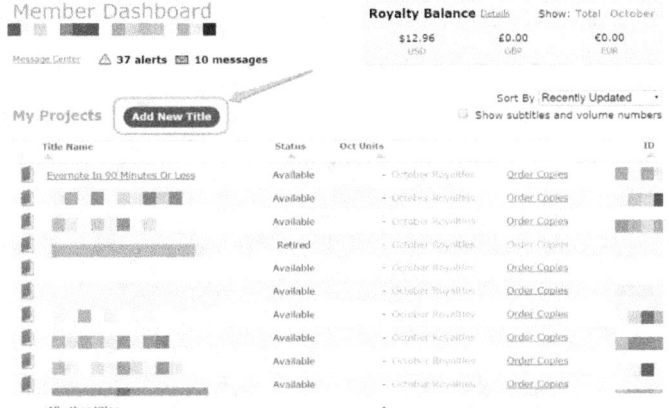

## Step 2

After you do that, you need to add the title (the title you put there isn't permanent, you can change it any time before submitting the files for the final review). Choose "Paperback" and also choose guided.

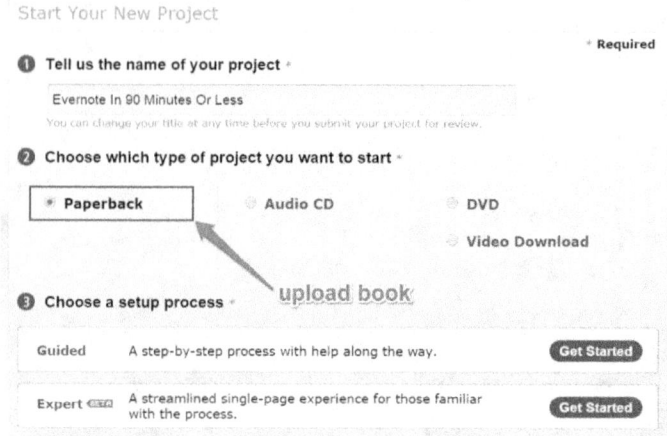

## *Step 3*

Choose a title, a subtitle, enter your name (the name of the author), and if necessary, add the title of a series and the volume number. Some of the fields are mandatory, whereas some are just optional (check the next photo attached).

Don't put anything in the Publication Date field because it will automatically be filled.

**What to do on this page:** Enter title information, including title and author. This information is associated with your book's ISBN and cannot be changed after you complete the review process.

* Required

| | |
|---|---|
| **Title** * | Evernote In 90 Minutes Or Less |
| **Subtitle** What's this? | Declutter and organize your life by going completely |

**Primary Author** *
What's this?

| Prefix | First Name / Initial | Middle Name / Initial | Last Name / Surname * | Suffix |
|---|---|---|---|---|
| | Ryan | | Stevens | |

**Add Contributors**
What's this?

Authored by ▼   **Add**

☐ This book is part of a series (What's this?)                              optional

| **Series Title** | | Volume | ▼ |
|---|---|---|---|

| **Edition number** What's this? | |
|---|---|

| **Language** * What's this? | English ▼ |
|---|---|

| **Publication Date** What's this? | |
|---|---|

**Save**   **Save & Continue**

## Step 4

All the physical books that you see in stores have one thing in common – the ISBN (International Standard Book Number). The ISBN codes are usually on the back of every book and are mandatory for finishing the process of publishing on CreateSpace.

You have 2 options: you assign your own ISBN if you already published your book elsewhere (and you have an existing one), or, if you want to use CreateSpace as your exclusive option, then choose *"Free CreateSpace-Assigned ISBN"*.

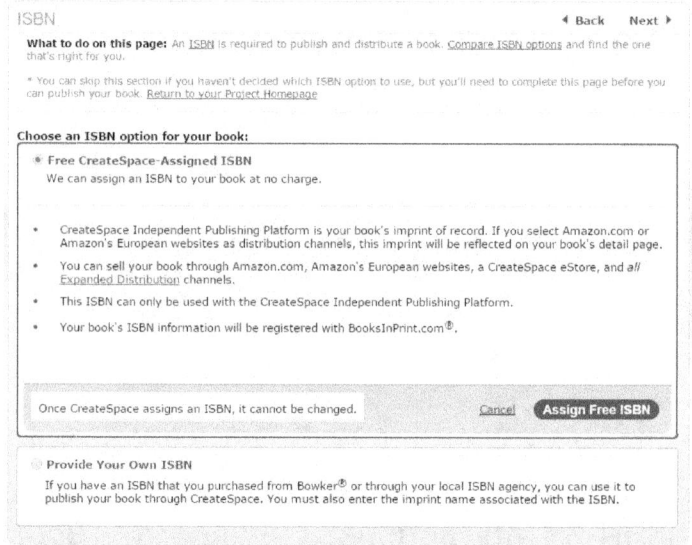

*Note – Once you choose the ISBN codes for your book, you can't change it. The only way to change what you've done is to retire*

*a title from CreateSpace and to re-upload it.*

## Step 5

Select your trim size. You have multiple options to choose from but I generally use just 2: 5 x 8 inches or 6 x 9 inches. To be honest, the 5 x 8 format is best if you have a book with less than 180-200 pages. I have seen dozens of books on Amazon with 23 pages on a 6 x 9 format, which is really awful. That's what I call a supersized pamphlet. However, what makes me sad is the fact that someone actually buys that.

I have been to a lot of bookstores and believe me, the most commonly used formats are 5 x 8 or 5.5 x 8 or similar. A 6 x 9 format is sometimes too big and it makes books look awkward. In my case, I use 5 x 8 for all my books as they all have 60 to 170 pages.

Even on Kindle, the way they count the pages isn't done properly. Amazon counts A4 pages (8.5 x 11 inches) and it's way too much for a book. I don't know what books you have seen, but I definitely haven't seen A4 books (except atlases or encyclopedias). So, to make readers understand the true page count of your book, it must be based on a real page count.

Here are all the formats provided by CreateSpace:

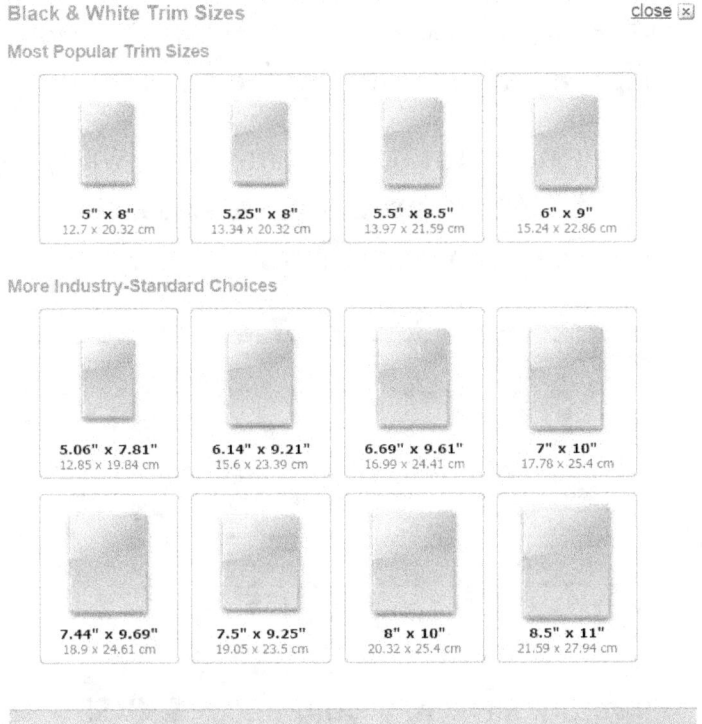

Black & White Trim Sizes                    close ⓧ

Most Popular Trim Sizes

| 5" x 8" | 5.25" x 8" | 5.5" x 8.5" | 6" x 9" |
| 12.7 x 20.32 cm | 13.34 x 20.32 cm | 13.97 x 21.59 cm | 15.24 x 22.86 cm |

More Industry-Standard Choices

| 5.06" x 7.81" | 6.14" x 9.21" | 6.69" x 9.61" | 7" x 10" |
| 12.85 x 19.84 cm | 15.6 x 23.39 cm | 16.99 x 24.41 cm | 17.78 x 25.4 cm |

| 7.44" x 9.69" | 7.5" x 9.25" | 8" x 10" | 8.5" x 11" |
| 18.9 x 24.61 cm | 19.05 x 23.5 cm | 20.32 x 25.4 cm | 21.59 x 27.94 cm |

Compare all sizes to 8.5" x 11" (PDF, 363k)          More Sizes

## *Step 6*

Upload the interior file. Make sure you have proofread your book and also make sure to format it properly. I highly advise you to hire professionals to do that. My place to go for those services is Fiverr. It's fast, easy, and relatively cheap.

If you have the money and you want to spend $199 on premium services, you can use CreateSpace's team to do that.

**Choose how you'd like to submit your interior:**

Upload your Book File

You can upload your work as a print-ready .pdf, .doc, .docx, or .rtf. Your page count will be detected and an automated print check will run once your upload is complete. You'll be able to see any issues online using the Interior Reviewer tool.

* Required

Interior File *                                        Browse

The following formats are accepted: pdf,doc,docx,rtf

Starting at $199

Talk with us about Professional Design Services

Let us design and format your manuscript. Our experienced team can help with fonts, margins, chapter headings, and other eye-catching details to enhance the professional appearance of your book.

I would say that you need $20-$50 to proofread and edit your book properly by using Fiverr.

When you upload your interior file, make sure to have a .docx or PDF file. You will have the best quality and fastest upload speeds from PDF formats, so use those. If you write your projects in Microsoft Word, save it as a PDF – Save As -> PDF format.

## *Step 7*

Let CreateSpace check your interior and see if you have any issues.

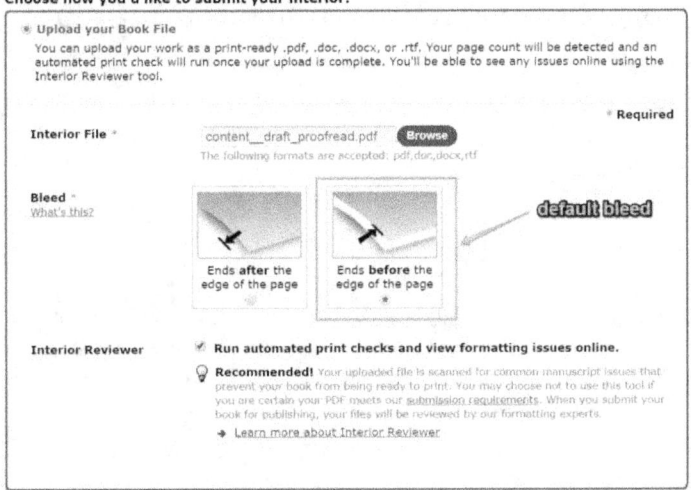

The most common issue is the pixel density of the pictures you insert. Generally, if you insert a picture with a dpi below 300, then it may appear blurry in the print book. Most of the photos (screenshots) from this book that you are reading have a dpi of 200-220, so if they appear blurry, I am sorry, there's nothing I can do to fix that even if I am using a Full HD display.

If you want to use a fancy font, don't forget to embed it within Microsoft Word.

Then, launch Interior Reviewer to check the issues. If you decide it's okay, you can exit and continue the process.

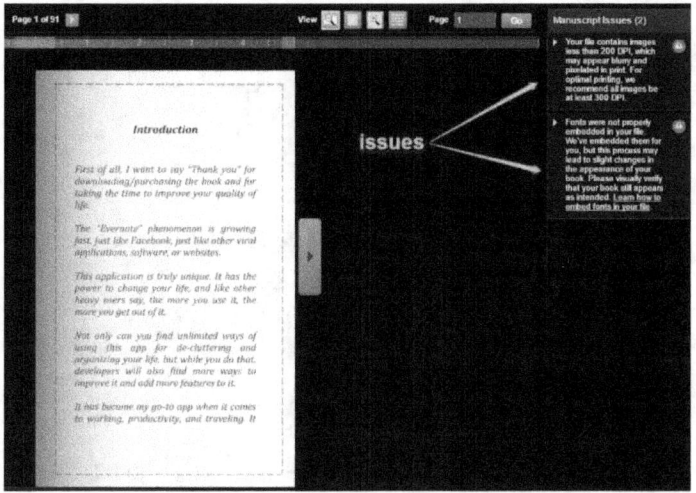

## Step 8

Upload your cover. A PDF file is mandatory for uploading the cover.

The PDF file needs to have the front, back, and spine of the book and it has to look like this:

You can use their free cover creator, but I find it too simple, too basic, and you can't customize many things.

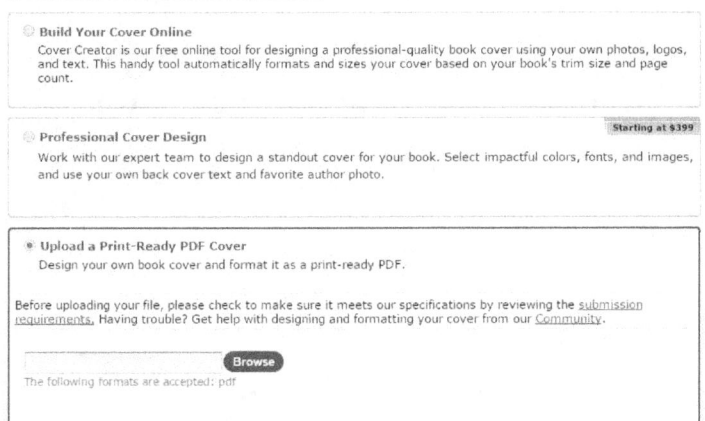

**2. Choose how to submit the cover of your book:**

Build Your Cover Online

Cover Creator is our free online tool for designing a professional-quality book cover using your own photos, logos, and text. This handy tool automatically formats and sizes your cover based on your book's trim size and page count.

Professional Cover Design    Starting at $399

Work with our expert team to design a standout cover for your book. Select impactful colors, fonts, and images, and use your own back cover text and favorite author photo.

Upload a Print-Ready PDF Cover

Design your own book cover and format it as a print-ready PDF.

Before uploading your file, please check to make sure it meets our specifications by reviewing the submission requirements. Having trouble? Get help with designing and formatting your cover from our Community.

Browse

The following formats are accepted: pdf

I design my covers on Fiverr – I pay between $20 and $40 and I get:

- A flat 2D cover (front) for Kindle
- A premium stock photo of my choice from Fotolia, Shutterstock, or iStockphoto.
- Front, back, and spine PDF cover for CreateSpace (you need to provide the number of pages, type of paper, if the interior is Black & White or Full Color, if you want the cover to be Glossy or Matte, etc.).

Also, don't forget to choose the type of the cover: Glossy or Matte. I tend to use both, but I have been using the Matte type more.

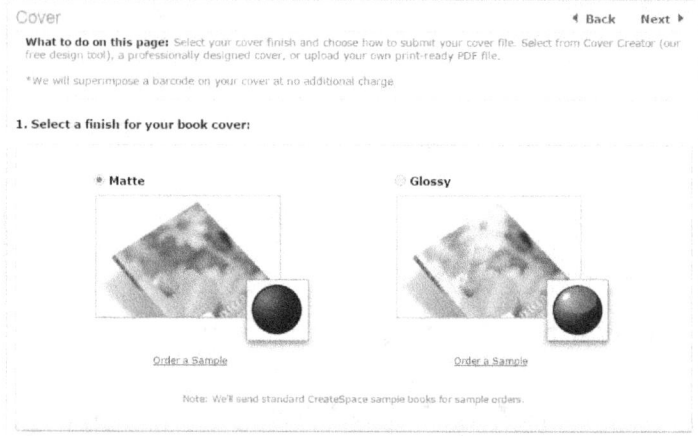

Of course, you can invest even $1,000 in an ultimate quality cover on 99designs, for example, or even more than that. I am just presenting the cheaper options and the ones that I use myself.

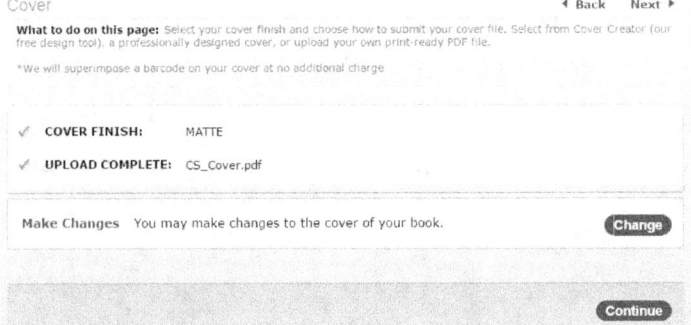

## Step 9

Submit your files for review. You need to wait between 12 and 24 hours until CreateSpace reviews your work. If the cover was properly formatted and your project meets all their requirements, you will be approved.

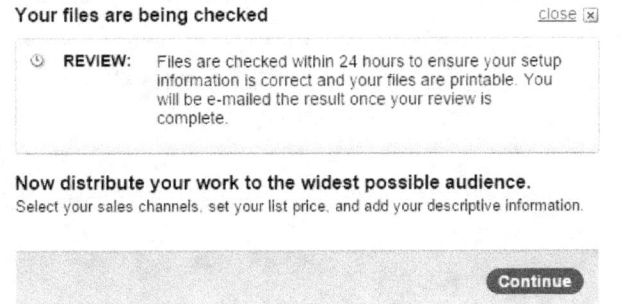

You can now have a small break or you can continue working on a few details until they send you the result – pricing, book description, keywords, channels, etc.

## *Step 10*

Choose your channels. You have 2 primary options: *Standard Distribution* and *Expanded Distribution.*

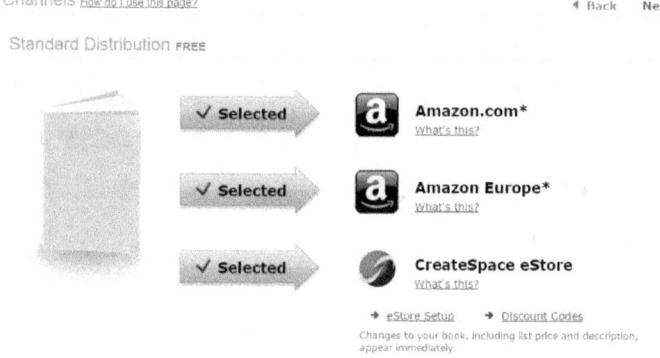

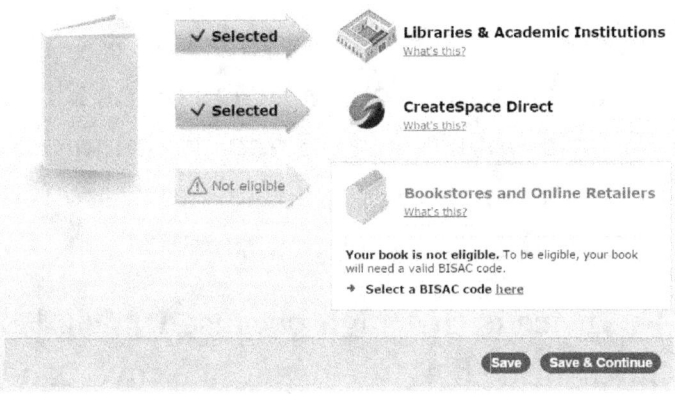

The last channel (libraries, bookstores, and online retailers) can be chosen once you choose the category of your book.

In my case, I chose Computers/Web/Content Management Systems. Soon after that, you can enroll in the last channel.

BISAC Category *          Computers / Web / Content          Choose...
What's this?             Management Systems

→ Enter a BISAC code

### *Step 11*

Choose the price of your book. The minimum price you can choose for Black & White books is $5.38 and the minimum for full color books is somewhere around $9.5 (higher costs for printing).

The price is that high because it includes the printing fees, the paper, the cover, and their commission. In that price, you get a royalty, but it's way too small. I generally tend to choose a price from $6.99 to $9.99, but it also depends on the price of the Kindle book.

If I have a book with 100 pages and it's priced at $2.99, I price the book at $7.99 or $8.99.

At the price of $7.99, you get a royalty of $2.64, while on Kindle, you get a $2.07 for a $2.99 book.

If you have more pages, the minimum price you can use increases. This usually happens after 150 pages.

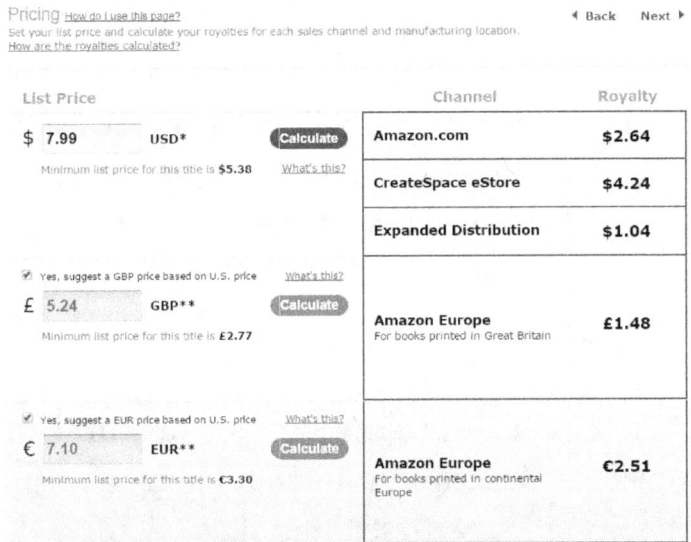

Unfortunately, you get a lower royalty for books sold in the EU or UK because VAT is included in the price and your commission decreases.

I recommend to use the Kindle Matchbook program – when someone purchases a print book from Amazon, that person gets the digital version for free or for a lower price (I use the free option).

A couple of times, I have spotted some mistakes in some of my books and I had to update the interior on both CreateSpace and Kindle. The print book won't update, but the Kindle one will, so make sure to use this feature, so everyone will be happy.

### *Step 12*

Write your description. Make sure to make a descriptive introduction of your book – it's the first thing that people will see and it has a great impact upon your future sales.

Write as much as possible and make sure that you don't have any errors in the description. Any tiny error will make people leave your page.

**Evernote In 90 Minutes Or Less**
By Ryan Stevens

**Description** *
What's this?

This application is truly unique. It has the power to change your life, and like other heavy users say, the more you use it, the more you get out of it.

Not only can you find unlimited ways of using this app for de-cluttering and organizing your life, but while you do that, developers will also find more ways to improve it and add more features to it.

It has become my go-to app when it comes to working, productivity, and traveling. It has become my all-in-one business application that helps me grow my entire business. All I have to say about it is that it has immense potential!!

In this guide, I will show you exactly what you need to know to use it properly – I will be concise, I will show you a few tricks, and I will illustrate the process of setting it up properly.

Maximum 4000 characters - 2649 characters remaining
Advanced users can use limited HTML instead of plain text to style and format their description

# Step 13

Choose your keywords carefully. Use tools such as Google Keyword Planner or Amazon Search bar, and see which words are the most frequently used.

Some say that keywords must be very long to include as many words as possible to describe a benefit or an advantage. I would rather say that they're wrong – you need 2-3 concise words that describe your book best. By using 2-3 words, you are increasing the keyword density and thus, you're increasing the chance of ranking your book higher in the searches.

CreateSpace allows you to use up to 5 keywords (20-25 characters per keyword), so be careful how you use them.

## Step 14

You will receive an email from CreateSpace in which they will tell you the final result – if your book meets their requirements.

If you see a "Congratulations" anywhere in your email (usually at the top), it means that you are good to go.

If something went wrong, try to fix any errors and resubmit your files until they meet their requirements.

Next, you need to go to your Member Dashboard and if everything is okay, you will see next to your title.

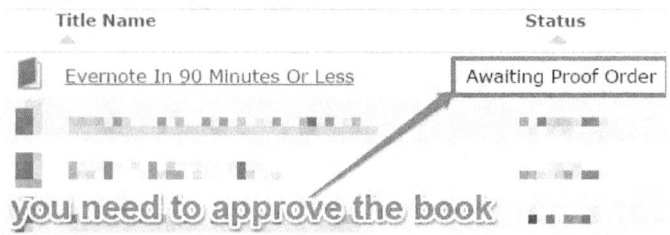

you need to approve the book

## *Step 15*

Click on your title. Take a look at the cover, it should be well arranged (centered).

Project Summary
**Evernote In 90 Minutes Or Less:** Declutter and organize your life by going completely paperless
Authored by Ryan Stevens

List Price: **$7.99**

**5" x 8"** (12.7 x 20.32 cm)
Black & White on White paper
96 pages

ISBN-13: **978-1517777937** (CreateSpace-Assigned)
ISBN-10: **1517777933**
BISAC: Computers / Web / Content Management Systems

This application is truly unique. It has the power to change your life, and like other heavy users say, the more you use it, the more you get out of it.

Not only can you find unlimited ways of using this app for de-cluttering and organizing your life, but while you do that, developers will also find more ways to improve it and add more features to it.

It has become my go-to app when it comes to working, productivity, and traveling. It has become my all-in-one business application that helps me grow my entire business. All I have to say about it is that it has immense potential!

In this guide...
➕ Entire Description

## *Step 16*

Proof your book. You need to enter their Digital Proofreader to make sure that your book is in perfect condition.

You are the one who makes the decision of approving it or not. Look for any errors and fix them before uploading the book – every mistake that you want to correct will cost you the time of resubmitting the book for review again.

Every time you update something or upload something new, you need to go through the whole process again, so try to make it good from the beginning.

Proof Your Book

**What to do on this page:**
Proofing your book will help you discover any formatting, grammar, or design issues within your files.

### Congratulations! Your files are printable.

✓ **REVIEW COMPLETE:** Your files have successfully passed our review process.

✎ **FIXED:** The interior contains transparency which is flattened during our processing and may result in a slight change in appearance.

⚠ **NOTED:** The interior contains images that are less than 200 DPI; these may appear blurry or pixelated when printed. For more information on image resolution, visit our Help page: https://www.createspace.com/Help/Index.jsp?orgId=00D300000001Sh9&id=50170000000Irmr

Proofing Options

View an online proof or order a physical copy to review your book. We recommend using a combination of both proofing options—you can use any combination of these features, in any order you choose.

▶ View a Digital Proof                                    Free

Use our Digital Proofer to review your book. This is a faster way to check your book before making it available for sale.

Click to expand

▶ Order a Printed Proof                    $2.15 each plus shipping and handling

Order a physical copy of your book to review. If you are new to publishing we strongly recommend selecting this option.

Click to expand

If you look carefully at the photo, you have the possibility to order units for which you only pay the printing fees + shipping. If you live in Europe like me, that would be really time consuming and expensive. I always go with the free option (Digital Proofreader).

Now, enter the proofreader and view your project.

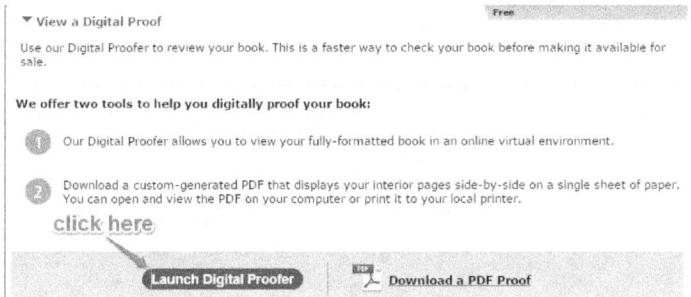

Take a closer look at my cover. Note the spine width, the ISBN codes and how everything is arranged.

Now, take a closer look at your book in 3D – spin it and look for any errors.

Click left and right arrows to spin, or click and drag the image to spin

◄     Spin ↻     ►

## *Step 17*

Exit the proofreader and hit the "Approve" button.

View an online proof or order a physical copy to review your book. We recommend using a combination of both proofing options—you can use any combination of these features, in any order you choose.

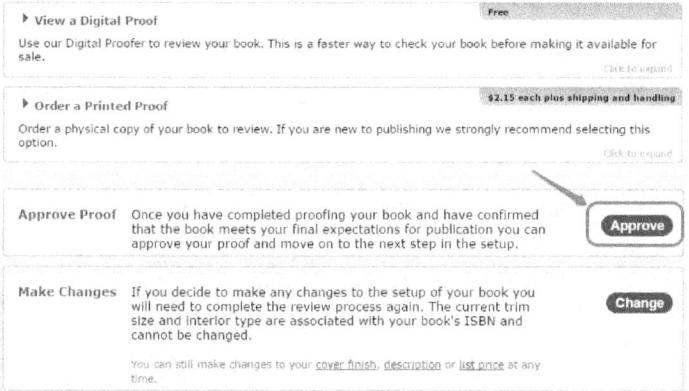

## Confirm Approval

Please confirm that you have completed proofing your book and that the book meets your final expectations for publication. Once you approve your proof it will become available for sale in the channels that you have selected.

Congratulations, you have successfully uploaded your project! It will be available on Amazon and on all the channels within 48 hours.

close ☒

# Congratulations!

**You've completed the setup of your book.**

Share your News

You can change your pricing, description information, and channels at any time in the **Distribute** section.

**Your book will be available in the following timeframes:**

Updates to your book will also appear in these timeframes.

- CreateSpace eStore: **Immediately**
- Amazon.com: **3-5 Business Days**
- Amazon Europe: **3-5 Business Days**
- Expanded Distribution channels: **6-8 Weeks**

💡 **Want to market your work?**

➜ Learn how to get started in our Marketing Center

☑ Give us your feedback        **Close Window**

In the next chapter, I will show you a few tricks to use before and after you start a new project.

# Chapter 5: Linking Your Kindle Book to CreateSpace

Most of the self-publishers don't know a little secret that helps even readers understand what's inside the book.

On Kindle, you have a standardized page count that is based on A4 format, whereas on CreateSpace, you have the format of a *real* book – 5 x 8 or 6 x 9 inches.

Let's face it, most of the books that you see have a compact form, so you need to update the book length of your Kindle book directly from CreateSpace.

## How?

Check out the photos below.

## Step 1

Sign in to your KDP account.

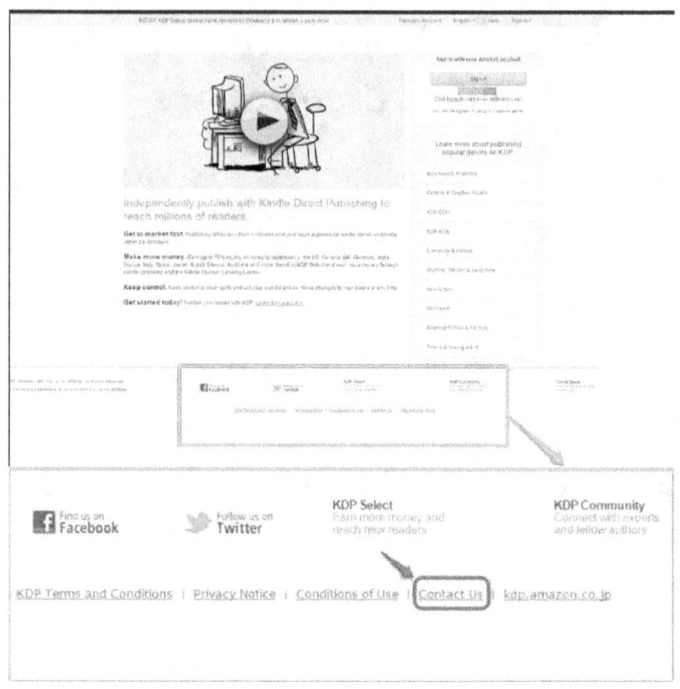

### Step 2

Go to the bottom of the page and click on the "Contact US" button.

### Step 3

Choose a random reason for contacting them and write in the message something similar to what I did.

## *Step 4*

Copy the ASIN and the ISBNs and include them in your message.

Hi,

I just uploaded a new title and I kindly ask you to link the print edition from CreateSpace to the digital version from Kindle. Make them a 2 in 1 on the same page. Also, please update the number of pages on Kindle from the print edition (Real page count).

ASIN: B016H4VHWW

ISBN-13: 978-1517777937 (CreateSpace-Assigned)
ISBN-10: 1517777933

Thanks in advance!

*i* Enter as much information as possible.

 Thank you! We've received your message. You should expect a response within 24 hours. In some cases our reply may take longer as we research your inquiry.

To get the ASIN of the book, go to the page of the Kindle book (on Amazon).

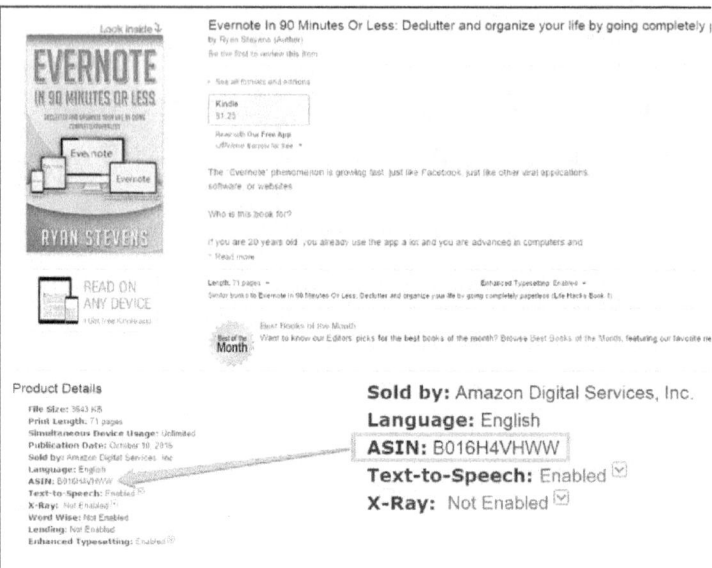

**Product Details**

File Size: 3643 KB
Print Length: 71 pages
Simultaneous Device Usage: Unlimited
Publication Date: October 10, 2015
Sold by: Amazon Digital Services, Inc.
Language: English
ASIN: B016H4VHWW
Text-to-Speech: Enabled
X-Ray: Not Enabled
Word Wise: Not Enabled
Lending: Not Enabled
Enhanced Typesetting: Enabled

**Sold by:** Amazon Digital Services, Inc.
**Language:** English
**ASIN:** B016H4VHWW
**Text-to-Speech:** Enabled
**X-Ray:** Not Enabled

For the ISBNs, go to CreateSpace, login, and click on the book (in the Member Dashboard).

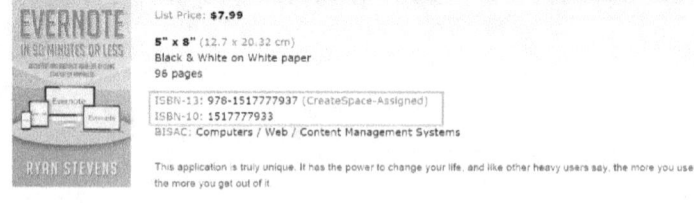

List Price: **$7.99**

**5" x 8"** (12.7 x 20.32 cm)
Black & White on White paper
96 pages

ISBN-13: 978-1517777937 (CreateSpace-Assigned)
ISBN-10: 1517777933
BISAC: Computers / Web / Content Management Systems

This application is truly unique. It has the power to change your life, and like other heavy users say, the more you use it, the more you get out of it.

## *Step 5*

Wait for Amazon KDP support to answer to your inquiry. They usually understand what you ask them and they manually link the CreateSpace book to the Kindle book and they also link the reviews (or combine them).

Here's what you should expect from Amazon:

Hello,

It will be a pleasure to assist you today.

I have manually linked the Kindle and physical versions of your title, "Evernote In 90 Minutes Or Less."

Please, keep in mind this change should appear on our website within 48 hours. However, it can take up to five days for customer reviews on any other editions to be linked to the Kindle edition.

Regarding your second request, I reviewed the current length of your title and updated it on our website to reflect a length of 96 pages. You should see the new information displayed online within 24 hours.

Thanks for using Amazon KDP.

## Step 6

Allow 48 hours to see the change – a 2 in 1 format on the same page – *Print Edition + Kindle Edition.*

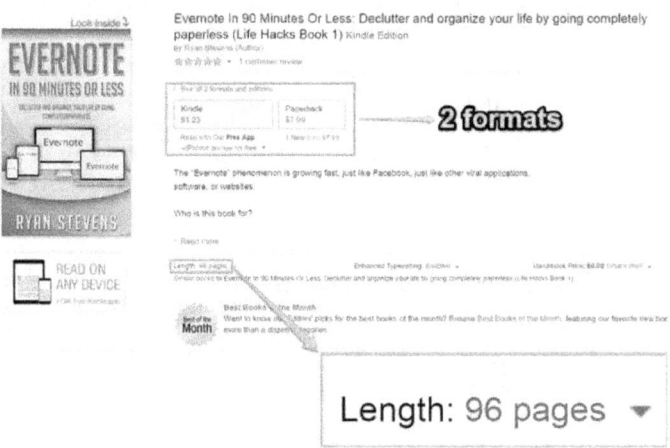

# Chapter 6: Become a CreateSpace Affiliate

*Before I explain the affiliate program, I want to let you know that I don't use any affiliate links in this book towards CreateSpace and for the moment, I am not an affiliate.*

To take advantage of the CreateSpace affiliate program, you firstly need a website or a blog dedicated to that topic. Right now, I am in the middle of the process of building one, so in the near future, I will sign up for their affiliate program as well.

### How Does It Work?

Very simple. You need to sign up for their program to place ads on your website and you will earn $8 for every new person who creates a new account (via your affiliate links or ads).

*Beware – don't tell your friends to create new accounts because they track everything and if they find out that you're scamming them, you will get banned as a member and as an affiliate. That means that you lose everything.*

Join the CreateSpace Affiliate Program Today!
Help us spread the word about CreateSpace to authors, filmmakers and musicians .. and get paid for doing so!

Here's the deal: We'll pay you $8 for every new CreateSpace member you refer to us!

**Here's how it works:**

1. Sign up **to become a CreateSpace affiliate.**
   We've teamed up with Commission Junction, a global leader in affiliate marketing, to make this process smooth and easy.
2. **Place CreateSpace ads on your website.**
   Choose from a variety of CreateSpace text links and banner ads to find the perfect ones to suit your audience.
3. **Earn money!**
   Earn $8 for every person who clicks through one of the CreateSpace ads on your site and creates a new CreateSpace account.

It's that easy! Join the CreateSpace Affiliate program today.

[ Join the Affiliate Program Now ]

You write a great blog post and make a review of CreateSpace and you can kindly tell people to sign up through your affiliate link if they want to start a CreateSpace self-publishing business.

Being nice and transparent is the best way to make money these days. I don't know much about you, but I had enough of fake marketers and scammers all over the Internet.

## Other Books by Ryan Stevens

*Amazon Associates*

*Kindle Publishing PRO*

*Entrepreneur Enhanced*

*Evernote in 90 Minutes or Less*

*More are on their way, I will update you soon.*

You are more than welcome to take a look at my blog – great posts, offers, and more! It's in process right now, but until it's completely ready, you can give a *Thumbs Up to my Facebook page – Entrepreneur Enhanced.*

## Write a review

*Your opinion matters!*

*Reviews are crucial for my business and also for improving myself and my books.*

*Share your thoughts with me and other customers by writing a short, concise review. It's up to you how you review it.*

*I constantly update my books every time they require attention. By receiving reviews, I will know exactly what I need to fix.*

# Last Word

*CreateSpace is a great way to make money as a self-publisher. It literally allows you to start from zero, it allows you to grow, and it isn't hard to understand at all.*

*All you need is persistence and dedication. If you have these great skills, then you're all set – I am more than sure that you will have success with it.*

*I want to sincerely thank you for purchasing this book and for taking the time to read it.*

*Feel free to contact me on my blog or Facebook Page if you have any questions. I am more than happy to answer.*

*Thank you,*

*Ryan*